The Spirit of Rejection:

Heal its Wounds, Restore Your Self-Esteem and Move on to Promotion

By Lenita Reeves

PurposeHouse Publishing

ASIN: B00QJ4EV42
ISBN: 0996364706

Unless otherwise indicated, all scriptural quotations are from the
King James Version of the Bible.

Scripture from New King James Version, Copyright © 1982 by
Thomas Nelson, Inc. All rights reserved.

Scripture from Amplified Bible, Copyright © 1987 by the Lockman
Foundation. (www.Lockman.org)

Scripture from the Message Bible, Copyright © 1993, 1994, 1995,
1996, 2000, 2001, 2002 by Eugene H. Peterson. All rights reserved.

Scripture from the New International Version, Copyright © 1973,
1978, 1984 by Biblica.

Scripture from the New Living Translation, Copyright © 1996,
2004 by Tyndale Charitable Trust.

Dedication

*To the chosen ones who have supported me through my season of
pain and accepted me and my ministry.*

Epigraph

"Reject the rejecter." — Author

Contents

Contents

Foreword

Conflict—picture it. Hear it inside of you and in your environment. What image(s) does it invoke? What does it stir in you? Conflict was the catalyst of this book. I have it to thank for provoking me to investigate what was going on inside of me and around me, for digging back into the nature and purpose of rejection and holding up a mirror to my thoughts, dispositions and behavior.

I found a conflict between giftedness (knowing you have something to offer) and rejection, between ability and acceptedness. But this time, instead of internalizing the pain or just getting angry I began to ask why? Why are people who are gifted, intelligent and anointed still rejected by the very people who need what they have to offer? In some cases, they don't value themselves and their internal thinking influences others' response to them. But in other cases, there are people with healthy self-esteem and self-concepts that are rejected for seemingly no good reason.

These observations beg answers to certain questions. Beyond just knowing that there is pain in the heart, what does the spirit of rejection actually do to your psyche, spirit and soul? How does it actually operate and what are the undetected side effects of its wounds? These were the burning questions that fueled my writing of this book. It is my prayer that within these pages you will find the answers and that Holy Spirit will illuminate the scriptures and examples and bring healing and peace to all who read.

Lenita Reeves

Acknowledgements

There are some revelations that come in the winter seasons of life—the sad, bad and mad seasons when we wonder when God will turn off the pressure spigot. The seasons when we expect the support of loved ones but instead their love flatlines. This book was written in one of those seasons; but, I thank God for those who stood with me during that time. My prayer is that God will honor the few faithful who were there in times of pain and supported me and my ministry. You know who you are and I sincerely want to thank you.

Introduction

*For the mouth of the wicked and the mouth of the
deceitful are opened against me: they have spoken
against me with a lying tongue. [3] They compassed me
about also with words of hatred; and fought against me
without a cause. [4] For my love they are my adversaries:
but I give myself unto prayer. [5] And they have rewarded
me evil for good, and hatred for my love...[22] For I am
poor and needy, and **my heart is wounded** within me.* –
Psalm 109:2-5, 22

Nothing wounds the heart like rejection. A potent weapon; it has
the power to dwarf greatness, discredit genius, disarm warriors
and damage relationships. If you think about it, almost every
person you know has had an encounter with rejection. As people
become more mobile (relocating more often), more isolated from
their families, and more hardened in their hearts, its prevalence
will likely increase. More than ever, the church must be equipped
to deal with rejection and bring healing to the bruised who have
come into her doors.

Because everyone is made in the image of God—who is love—
each of us has an innate desire to be loved and show love. When
expressions of love are returned with rejection it is an anti-God
reaction. David details his own similar experience in Psalm 109.
His response was violent prayer.

Yet, giving ourselves to prayer is only one necessary step to
dealing with rejection. Simple medical practice helps us
understand (in the natural) other vital steps to deal with
rejection's wounds. For example, webmd.com offers these
simple steps for dealing with a bleeding wound: apply pressure
to the wound to stop bleeding, clean the wound and finally,
protect the wound. Each of these steps has application to dealing
with rejection.

1. Apply pressure:
    a. In the spiritual, applying pressure is resisting the devil's spirit of rejection. To resist is to apply pressure against [an object] in order to move in an opposite direction or prevent it from moving any further. The scripture tells us to resist the devil and he will flee from us (James 4:7). To be victorious, believers need to learn to recognize and resist the spirit of rejection. This book is designed to equip you to do that.
2. Clean the wound:
    a. After resisting the enemy or applying pressure to the wound to stop the bleeding, you then need to cleanse the wound(s). This involves two steps:
        i. Remove any debris from the wound; meaning, cast out the spirits of rejection, fear of rejection and self-rejection. The prayers included in this book will lead you through casting out these foul spirits.
        ii. Cleanse your soul with the water of the word. Ephesians 5:26 says, Jesus cleanses His bride with the washing of water by the word. It is necessary to apply the Word of God to cleanse the wounds of rejection. You will find relevant scriptures as you read through this book to help you do just that.
3. Protect the wound:
    a. You are transformed by the renewing of your mind. Understanding and believing what God says about your self-image, self-concept and self-esteem is a hedge of protection against attacks of rejection in your life. 1 Peter 1:13 says gird up the loins of our minds; in other words, keep your mind strengthened and built up with the truth of who you are in Christ. The last chapter of this

book is devoted to exploring the 3 Ss: self-image, self-concept and self-esteem.

In addition to these essential steps to dealing with rejection, this book includes reflection questions at the end of each chapter. The questions can be used for discussion in small groups or individually with journaling. As you read these pages, may rejection be eradicated from your life and/or may you learn how to help others evict this illegal tenant. God richly bless you.

The Spirit of Rejection:

Heal its Wounds, Restore Your Self-Esteem and Move on to Promotion

1   The Nature and Purpose of Rejection

Reject [v. ri-jekt; n. ree-jekt] to spurn | to kick or trample with the foot | to refuse to accept | also intransitively to disappear

It's the end of the workday but not the end of the pressure. Mother has furiously unpacked the groceries and in corresponding rapid fashion, changed her clothes in preparation to cook. As she lays her clothes on the bed, she glances across the room. A family picture has fallen sideways. "This room looks like a tornado blew through it," she thinks. In frustration and for lack of time, she refuses to acquiesce to the urge to put things in order.

On her way to kitchen, she trips over the toys in the hallway. She almost screams but manages to keep her composure. Just as she gets the first pot on the stove, her youngest son runs into the kitchen.

"Mommy, mommy see my--"

"Sit down. What makes you think I want to see that right now? You're just like your daddy: you'll never be anything. Just go sit down."

If you've ever witnessed a mother talking to her child this way and something inside you cringed, you've experienced the terrible effects of rejection. Even when experienced second-hand, rejection feels like a spiritual punch in the gut or spit in the face. Undoubtedly, if that child could make himself disappear he would.

But you and I don't just experience rejection second-hand. It is a force that you (or someone close to you) are intimately acquainted with, whether you know how to deal with it or not. What's worse is rejection comes in varied packages. You may have been cast out of the in crowd as a child at school, teenager in high school or even as an adult in church. You may have never known the love of your biological father, suffered from the negative words of a frustrated, overworked single mom, set aside because you were overweight or rejected because of the color of your skin. Whatever the case, the debilitating impacts of rejection do not discriminate, metaphorically coming in all forms, shapes and sizes.

Its impacts are so detrimental because they attack your sense of identity. Rejection first attacks your belief in *who you are* in order to negatively affect *your ability to do* what you are called to do. Think about that same mother and child as an example: how would his mother's words of rejection affect his ability to see himself as a beloved son (who he is) and to do the things a son is supposed to do for his mother (ability to do)? Once you begin to doubt who you are, your ability to do is paralyzed.

You cannot be something by doing something, but rather who you are determines what you do. Paul did not say, "I do what I do by the grace of God," but he did say, "I am what I am by the grace of God" (1 Corinthians 15:10).[1]

> *Rejection first attacks your belief in who you are in order to negatively affect your ability to do what you are called to do.*

Even Paul, the writer of over two-thirds of the New Testament experienced rejection. However, Paul was able to overcome it and accomplish what he did because he was assured of who he

---

[1] Pitts, Michael. 2002. Don't Curse Your Crisis. M.A.P.S. Institute, Inc. p. 33

was—he was assured that God had called him to be an apostle and that his assignment was to take the gospel to the gentiles.

During Paul's time, there were many who were still not convinced that God could touch gentiles, so his assignment was nothing less than controversial. It would have been easy for him to give up and walk away. His assignment required him to breakthrough prejudice, traditions of circumcision, unbelief that the Holy Spirit could touch gentiles and his past reputation as a murderer. Even when the other apostles rejected him and conflict ensued between him and Peter, Paul was able to persevere because who knew who [God said] he was. Similarly, the Bible declares in Daniel 11:32b, but the people that *do know their God* shall be strong, and do exploits. Your ability to know God has a direct impact on your ability to know who God has called you to be (to know your true self) and to do exploits or great works.

So, it is important to understand that rejection fights against your belief in who you are and indirectly your ability to know God and do what you are called to do.

How does the enemy accomplish this? Let's look at the nature and purpose(s) of rejection and his tactics will become clearer.

The Nature and Purpose(s) of Rejection

First, know that rejection is a spirit.

Rejection is a Spirit

*2 Timothy 1:7 says, For God hath not given us the **spirit** of fear; but of power, and of love, and of a sound mind.*

At its base level, the spirit of rejection is a cousin to what the scripture calls the spirit of fear. People often experience rejection as the *fear of* being rejected. It stands to reason that if fear is a spirit, the fear of rejection is also a spirit.

Here is another example from scripture:

God sent a spirit of ill will between Abimelech and the men of Shechem; and the men of Shechem dealt treacherously with Abimelech – Judges 9:23

There is something called a spirit of ill will and it was sent specifically to cause people to deal treacherously with one another. This example lets us know that spirits carry out specific assignments and that one of their assignments can be to turn people against each other or, cause them to reject one another.

In addition, there are some demon spirits that Jesus encountered that were not specifically named in scripture but they were still demon spirits.

Now in the synagogue there was a man who had a spirit of an unclean demon. – Luke 4:33

The passage in Luke 4 goes on to detail the demon crying out and Jesus subsequently casting out the unclean demon. We don't know whether this demon was a demon of rejection, sickness or anything else unclean—all we know is that it was unclean—and rejection is certainly unclean. Rejection is a spirit.

---

*It stands to reason that if **fear** is a spirit, the **fear** of rejection is also a spirit.*

Rejection has four primary purposes

So understand that rejection is carried out by a spirit and the rejection you have or are experiencing has four primary, specific purposes; to cripple:

1. Your ability to know God intimately as a loving Father
2. Your belief in and understanding of your true identify
3. Your ability to know and love others
4. Others' ability to receive God's message through you

Purpose #1: Cripple your ability to know God intimately

Draw nigh to God, and he will draw nigh to you... -- James 4:8a

For ye have not received the spirit of bondage again to fear; but ye have received the Spirit of adoption, whereby we cry, Abba, Father. -- Romans 8:15

A Father's love both be received and given. Meaning, both parties—father and daughter or father and son—have a responsibility to extend themselves to the other, to reciprocate love and affection. If you don't open your hands to receive a gift, no matter how hard the giver tries, he or she can't give it to you. So the Father can (and does) love you but if the fear and wounds of rejection cause you to keep your hands closed, you won't experience His love. This is the *bondage again to fear* of which Romans 8:15 speaks. It's a bondage—slavery, subjection to evil control, involuntary servitude—that keeps you in servitude to fear and rejection. It keeps you from receiving the very thing you need; keeping you closed up from the one person you should never be afraid to open yourself to. You must understand that the devil's primary purpose for the attack of the spirit of rejection is to keep you from experiencing the Father's love.

You can't be guarded/defensive and draw close to God (or anyone) at the same time.

Sadly, rejection cripples both our ability to receive the Father's love and to pursue it. There is an African parable that says, "If you've been bitten by a snake when you see a worm you'll run." Rejection has a similar affect. If you've been bruised (bitten) by rejection you'll likely have a tendency to run or try to defend yourself at the first sight of it and to withdraw from others to protect yourself from it. This inadvertently effects your ability to *draw nigh* to God. You can't be guarded/defensive and draw close to God (or anyone) at the same time.

Purpose #2: Cripple your belief and understanding of your true identity

Ephesians 1:5-7
5 Having predestinated us unto the adoption of children by Jesus Christ to himself, according to the good pleasure of his will, 6 To the praise of the glory of his grace, wherein he hath made us accepted in the beloved. 7 In whom we have redemption through his blood, the forgiveness of sins, according to the riches of his grace;

Ephesians 1:5-7 (The Living Bible)
5 His unchanging plan has always been to adopt us into his own family by sending Jesus Christ to die for us. And he did this because he wanted to! 6 Now all praise to God for his wonderful kindness to us and his favor that he has poured out upon us because we belong to his dearly loved Son. 7 So overflowing is his kindness toward us that he took away all our sins through the blood of his Son, by whom we are saved;

Our self-image, self-concept (identity) and self-esteem are derived from our understanding of God as Father—as source. Your Father is your source, your *abba* and from where you proceed forth. When we embrace the truth that we are created in His image and likeness and that we have been created with limitless creative power as speaking spirits, we understand and grasp what should be the true foundation of our self-image and self-concept. If the enemy can damage your self-image through rejection, he can prevent you from walking in confidence and weaken your assurance that you are accepted by your source, your Father. In the same way that an appliance cannot function if not properly connected to a power source, when our connection to our source, our Father, is weakened, we function less effectively.

Even in the natural, children who have a good relationship with their fathers and see their fathers as loving and supportive are more self-confident. When there is damage to the father-child relationship, the child's self-image and self-esteem suffer. The same is true for your spiritual relationship with God the Father. When you are assured of His love and are free of any feeling that He is against you or mad at you, you are more confident and empowered to fulfill His will.

With this knowledge, the enemy uses the spirit of rejection to inflict emotional and spiritual wounds.

Psalm 109:22
[22] *For I am poor and needy, and my heart is wounded within me.*

Psalm 109:22 lets us know that the human heart (or spirit) can be wounded. Bruised soldiers are less effective in battle. Similarly, if the enemy can bruise you with rejection, causing you to question your identity and question the Father's love, he knows that you'll be less effective in your purpose and assignment. Consider this: why would God go through the trouble of predestinating you, writing your days in the volume of the books, creating and forming you with a divine purpose just to reject you?

Rejection can cause you to limp into your destiny rather than walk confidently into it, if you make it at all. One meaning of rejection is to spurn (Strongs3988 Hebrew) or to kick or trample with the foot. This give new meaning to the slang phrase "kick to the curb." It also paints a visual picture that rejection is like kicking someone in the leg to the extent that you cause them to limp. This is why rejection cannot be taken lightly. It must be dealt with as the dangerous enemy that it is because its purpose is to cripple you in *your purpose*.

Purpose #3: Cripple your ability to know and love others

Proverbs 18:24
A man that hath friends must shew himself friendly: and there is a friend that sticketh closer than a brother.

In the same way that God tells you to draw close to Him and He in turn will draw close to you, the nature of friendship is also reciprocal. Proverbs 18:24 says that if you would have friends, you must also shew yourself friendly. In other words, you have to open up and make an effort to develop friendships. If you are bruised by rejection and afraid to open up or take the risk of being rejected, you'll be hard pressed to develop friendships. So rejection perpetuates a vicious cycle—you want to be accepted but you are too bruised to show yourself friendly remaining isolated and alone.

Purpose #4: Cripple others' ability to receive God's message through you

Mark 6:1-5
And he went out from thence, and came into his own country; and his disciples follow him. ² And when the sabbath day was come, he began to teach in the synagogue: and many hearing him were astonished, saying, From whence hath this man these things? and what wisdom is this which is given unto him, that even such mighty works are wrought by his hands? ³ Is not this the carpenter, the son of Mary, the brother of James, and Joses, and of Juda, and Simon? and are not his sisters here with us? And they were offended at him. ⁴ But Jesus, said unto them, A

prophet is not without honour, but in his own country, and among his own kin, and in his own house. ⁵ And he could there do no mighty work, save that he laid his hands upon a few sick folk, and healed them.

What a crime—people who could have been set free, healed and released into their destinies did not encounter the touch of the master all because of rejection. The scripture says that they were offended at him—can you imagine?

Sometimes it's as if people are offended at you without a cause; you haven't done anything to them. You just show up and they are offended, which means they have rejected you in their minds and hearts and stumble at the thought of receiving you or what you have to say.

Interestingly enough, in the same way that one meaning of rejection is to kick as if to cripple, one meaning of being offended is to cause to stumble. Sadly those who stumbled at the thought of receiving Jesus (and you for that matter) didn't even know that that their offense was keeping them from their own deliverance. Sometimes folk think that by looking down on you they are hurting you but in the end they are hurting themselves and everyone else who was destined for deliverance.

Chapter Conclusion

In summary, the destructive purposes and effects of rejection are threefold; you turn away from God, from yourself and from others, creating a vicious cycle of isolation and rejection. In addition, the enemy can influence others to reject you in order to prevent them from receiving what God wants to say through you.

It is possible to recognize these destructive purposes in your life. Perhaps when you meet new people you are guarded? Or in groups when others are conversing and disclosing details about their lives, families or challenges, maybe you are the one who talks the least for fear of what they might think of you?

Have you given up on the idea that you'll have a circle of trusted friends and as a result, opt to be alone? Do you avoid gatherings (family, church, or work)? Do people comment that you are hard to get to know?

If your answers to any of these questions is yes, it's okay. Identifying rejection is the first step to being able to resist it. This is where the journey to healing begins. By answering the following reflection questions, you'll identify other ways that rejection has been at work in your life and then, address them in prayer.

For maximum benefit, please answer the following questions in an individual journal and/or in a group discussion setting.

1.) Consider the definition of rejection presented at the beginning of the chapter.
    a. Do you agree with this definition and why?
    b. How else would you describe what rejection feels like?

2.) Has rejection effected your ability to know God intimately as a loving Father?
    a. If so how?
    b. What steps can (or do) you take to draw nigh unto God?

3.) Has rejection effected your belief and/or understanding of your identity in Christ?
    a. If so how?
        i. Is there anyone who can help you/encourage you in this area and why do you think they are able to help you?
    b. If you have not been effected in this area, how would you advise/encourage others who have?

4.) Has rejection effected your ability to initiate and maintain healthy relationships with others?
    a. If so, how?
        i. Are there any people in particular you feel might be responsible for your sense of rejection and why?
    b. If you have not been effected in this area, how would you advise/encourage others?

5.) Do you think God would go through the trouble of predestinating you, writing your days in the volume of the books, creating and forming you with a divine purpose just to reject you?

    a. Why do you think people feel that He would?

    b. What does Ephesians 1:5-7 say God's plan was all along? What else can we learn from Ephesians 1:57? (see page 19)

Prayer

Father, your name is holy and I thank you for who you are. In the name of Jesus, I thank you that you have predestined me and the truth is, according to 1 John 4:18 that you love me with a perfect love that casts out all fear. This means that fear and rejection are illegal tenants in my life. So in the name of Jesus and by the authority of Jesus, I resist the spirit of fear, the spirit of the fear of rejection, the spirit of self-rejection and the spirit of rejection. I cast them out of my life in the name of Jesus. Father God, I loose your love, your acceptance and your peace in my life.

I command the spirits of fear and spirits of rejection to be arrested. I terminate your assignment and I command my unconditional release. You will not carry out any assignment in my life henceforth and forever more. Go to the place of divine appointment.

I command unclean, foul spirits to leave my house and my life. I evict you. You are evicted by divine authority. I throw you out of my life and my house in the name of Jesus!

Father I receive your love and your healing.

Amen.

2 The Lord knows what rejection feels like

Reject [v. ri-jekt; n. ree-jekt] forsake | cease | destitute |frail | he that forebeareth the precedeing

> *"I had one highly experienced deliverance minister tell me that spirits of rejection are among some of the most common demons that he has encountered throughout his ministry." – Robert L.[2]*

Having explored the nature and purpose of rejection, you can now appreciate why it is one of the enemy's frequently used, "go-to" weapons. Rejection is so common yet so dangerous. As evidenced in Hosea 4 and Isaiah 53, even our Father God and Lord Jesus know what rejection feels like. Hosea lays out God's claims against Israel and Judah and declares that their sinful state is a result of not acknowledging God and his laws.

> *Hosea 4:6*
> *My people are destroyed for lack of knowledge. Because you have rejected knowledge, I also will reject you from being priest for Me; because you have forgotten the law of your God, I also will forget your children. (NKJV)*

In Hosea 4:1-5, God issues indictments against the people, the prophets and the priests and each claim is a claim of sin—specifically not knowing or acknowledging God and His ways. So in Hosea 4:6, God issues judgment to the priests stating that, "because you refuse to know me I will also refuse to allow you and your children to be priests to me." In other words, God is saying that He will reject them and their children from being priest or, cause their line/lineage *to cease or disappear* from the priesthood.

---

[2] http://www.greatbiblestudy.com/rejection.php

This reveals another meaning of rejection; to treat someone like they don't exist, *to cease to acknowledge or to treat as if they have disappeared.* God's rejection is the ultimate rejection but He only rejects us if we refuse to acknowledge Him and refuse to turn away from our sin.

This passage, (or book of Hosea) like no other book in the Bible shows how intimately God is acquainted with rejection. He knows what it feels like; for He likened His children to an unfaithful wife—even a whore, to demonstrate how Israel had betrayed Him by following after strange, foreign gods.

While each of us have experienced rejection, few of us have done so after sacrificing our only, dear son to die for someone. God, having suffered the ultimate sacrifice for Israel, slaying His only son before the foundation of the world and bringing them out of Egypt, is now betrayed by the very people He sacrificed everything for—and yet, He remains faithful to them. When we consider the gravity of the situation, such love is hard to comprehend. While you and I would likely have given up on such ungrateful people, God remained faithful to Israel (to us) and saw them through to the fulfillment of the new covenant. If you ponder this, you would see that God doesn't just have a little compassion from time to time: He *is* love.

When you examine the state of Israel during the time of the writing of the book of Hosea, you see that God's description of them as a harlot is justified. While you and I have encountered the miracle working power of God, few of us have seen a river or sea part its waters with our own eyes or much less, had a great grand parent who saw it and told us stories about it.

Most likely, you have never experienced physical slavery for yourself and then been delivered from the hands of your harsh taskmaster by a sovereign move of God. But these are people who grew up on these stories and who could, first-hand, relate to experiencing God as a delivering battle winner and redeemer. Yet, they still betrayed their God. And yes, He still loved them. If you think of this in light of Romans 8, which says, nothing can separate us from the love of God, you get a better picture of God's love for you as an individual. Hallelujah!

Romans 8:35, 38-39
35 Who shall separate us from the love of Christ? shall tribulation, or distress, or persecution, or famine, or nakedness, or peril, or sword?...38 For I am persuaded, that neither death, nor life, nor angels, nor principalities, nor powers, nor things present, nor things to come, 39 Nor height, nor depth, nor any other creature, shall be able to separate us from the love of God, which is in Christ Jesus our Lord.

What a wonderful revelation of His love. If a God who experienced rejection from His own, could in turn love them, so can you. Selah.

> *1 Samuel 10:19*
> *And ye have this day rejected your God, who himself saved you out of all your adversities and your tribulations; and ye have said unto him, Nay, but set a king over us. Now therefore present yourselves before the Lord by your tribes, and by your thousands.*

1 Samuel 10:18-19 is another example of how God's own people rejected Him. God knows what rejection feels like.

> *18 And said unto the children of Israel, Thus saith the LORD God of Israel, I brought up Israel out of Egypt, and delivered you out of the hand of the Egyptians, and out of the hand of all kingdoms, and of them that oppressed you: 19 And ye have this day rejected your God, who himself saved you out of all your adversities and your tribulations; and ye have said unto him, Nay, but set a*

king over us. Now therefore present yourselves before the LORD by your tribes, and by your thousands.

One of the most hurtful things about this passage is that God reminds the children of Israel of what He has done for them. It's as if God is saying, "how is that I can do all of this for you and you still reject me?" You can sense the hurting heart of a loving Father.

So whether you are rejected by strangers or those for whom you have given your last dime, God knows what it feels like. He was rejected by those for which He poured out His heart and gave of Himself. The scripture says God Himself saved Israel out of all her adversities and tribulations and yet they still wanted a king over them.

Isaiah 53:3
He is despised and rejected of men; a man of sorrows, and acquainted with grief: and we hid as it were our faces from him; he was despised, and we esteemed him not.

Our Lord Jesus also experienced utter rejection. Isaiah 53 tells us that He was despised, rejected, full of sorrows, acquainted with grief, was not esteemed and that people hid their faces from him, or in other words, turned their backs on him. He was innocent, yet He suffered all of this rejection for our sakes; so that you and I would be free from the just judgment of sin. As He journeyed to the cross, people spat at Him, pulled his beard and rent his garments.

Again, though you and I have suffered rejection, not many of us have experienced it at the level that our Lord and Savior did—for our sakes, nonetheless. In all of this pain, suffering and rejection, our Lord was still able to say, "Father forgive them for they know not what they do." The truth that perfect love casts out all fear is not just for our own deliverance; but also to overcome the power of rejection by you loving your rejecter. You and I rejected the Father but He still showed us love and it broke down the wall of sin that was separating us from the Father.

In the same way, you and I can love those who reject us and spitefully use us.

> *Matthew 5:44-45*
> *[44] But I say unto you, Love your enemies, bless them that curse you, do good to them that hate you, and pray for them which despitefully use you, and persecute you;*
> *[45] That ye may be the children of your Father which is in heaven: for he maketh his sun to rise on the evil and on the good, and sendeth rain on the just and on the unjust.*

This does not negate the potency of your pain but lets you know that you serve a God and Savior who have also endured such pain and require you to move past it. "How?" you ask. You have to love your way past it just like they did. "But how do you do that?" you ask. Take a look at the Message version of this passage for greater insight.

> [43-47] "You're familiar with the old written law, 'Love your friend,' and its unwritten companion, 'Hate your enemy.' I'm challenging that. I'm telling you to love your enemies. Let them bring out the best in you, not the worst. When someone gives you a hard time, respond with the energies of prayer, for then you are working out of your true selves, your God-created selves. This is what God does. He gives his best—the sun to warm and the rain to nourish—to everyone, regardless: the good and bad, the nice and nasty. If all you do is love the lovable, do you expect a bonus? Anybody can do that. If you simply say hello to those who greet you, do you expect a medal? Any run-of-the-mill sinner does that.

This passage reveals two important keys to loving your way past the rejection of others:

1.) Let them bring out the best in you not the worst.

2.) Respond with the energies of prayer.

These keys are also reinforced in Roman 12:19-21:

> Dearly beloved, avenge not yourselves, but rather give place unto wrath: for it is written, Vengeance is mine; I will repay, saith the Lord. [20] Therefore if thine enemy hunger, feed him; if he thirst, give him drink: for in so doing thou shalt heap coals of fire on his head. [21] Be not overcome of evil, but overcome evil with good.

Remember, you are not responsible for others rejecting you but you are responsible for how your respond. God says that we are to be intentional in our response, intentionally responding with love rather than hate and by so doing heaping coals of fire on your rejecter's head(s). Could it be possible that your rejecter is a tool to bring out the best in you—to bring out the love nature of God from inside you? Remember that God was rejected by His own but responded in love, when you also respond in love the scripture says you are perfect like your Father God. Hosea 4 and 1 Samuel 10 show us that the bleeding heart can indeed love. It is possible to love out of pain and be perfect in the daunting face of rejection. Our Father has shown us this example.

You are not responsible for others rejecting you but you are responsible for how your respond.

How is that Jesus walked with Judas those three years knowing that his [Judas's] assignment was betrayal? Jesus knew that ultimately, Judas was just playing his part. How can God prepare a table before you without the presence of enemies? If you can come to realize that your rejecters are simply playing their part, you can view them from a perspective that is not personal and in turn respond to them in a way that doesn't take what they are doing personal.

The second key from Matthew 5 is to respond with the energies of prayer. The prayer of Christ while suffering in pain on the cross, "Father forgive them for they know not what they do" is a great example of how to respond with the energies of prayer.

It is at first difficult to pray for someone who has hurt you; but at the same time, it is difficult to stay mad at someone you pray for. While David prayed violent prayers against his enemies, Jesus commands us to bless our enemies and not curse them. It's hard to swallow; but if anyone knows what he's talking about it is Jesus.

> *It is at first difficult to pray for someone who has hurt you; but at the same time, it is difficult to stay mad at someone you pray for.*

A similar principle was put into action in the life of Job. His so-called, three friends had lots of misguided things to say until Jehovah personally addressed them and set them in their place. Nonetheless, the scripture declares that the Lord turned Job's captivity when he [Job] prayed for the three friends.

> *Job 42:10*
> *And the Lord turned the captivity of Job, when he prayed for his friends: also the Lord gave Job twice as much as he had before.*

Instead of using your energy to harbor anger; use that energy in prayer. When you sow the righteous seed of prayer for your enemies you release a certain "Christ energy." An energy of the Spirit that has the force to overcome evil with its good. Grudges, resentment and feelings of ill will break within you when you pray for your enemies and those who have molested, scandalized or spitefully used you.

It is comforting to know that we have a high priest that can be touched with the feeling our infirmities. He experienced rejection but responded in perfection—in love. He expects the same of us. You can love yourself out of the rejection and by doing so prove that you are child of the most high God. Loving those who are lovely is no test—it is loving those who reject us that makes us like God. When subjected to rejection-tainted relationships, focus on two things:

1.) Determine to let it bring the best out of you—not the worst.
2.) Focus your energies on prayer for those who are rejecting you.

Be reminded that if Jesus could love Judas and God could still love Israel even after they played the harlot, you can also respond in love when rejected.

For maximum benefit, please answer the following questions in an individual journal and/or in a group discussion setting.

1.) Revisit 1 Samuel 10:18-19. What do these verses tell you about how God felt?

2.) In this chapter, another meaning of rejection was presented; to treat someone like they don't exist, *to cease to acknowledge or to treat as if they have disappeared.* In what ways do we treat God like this? Why?

3.) God responded in love when rejected. Revisit Romans 12:19-21. What steps can you take to respond in love when rejected?

Prayer

Heavenly Father, I acknowledge your holiness and thank you for who you are. My prayer is for your grace to love my rejecters. According to your word, your strength is made perfect in weakness. I confess my weakness when it comes to forgiveness and loving my enemies and I pray that your strength, grace and divine enablement will be activated in my life. I declare that any rejection I encounter will bring out the best in me and not the worst.

By your grace, I will focus my energies in prayer instead of negative activities. Right now, I bless my enemies and I pray for those who are spitefully using me. I sow a seed of righteousness in prayer, in the name of Jesus.

I receive your love and your healing.

Amen.

3   Rejection is a Reflection of the Rejecter

Have you ever read a job description that detailed a position that was perfect for you? You gained excitement and courage with each sentence you read; thinking to yourself, "I can do this job!" Suddenly, you reach the bottom of the description and— smack—the job requires a PhD, which you don't have. Your balloon of hope deflates and the PhD is a wall of rejection erected unexpectedly in your face.

Jesus experienced a similar wall of rejection from those in His hometown. They thought, he doesn't have a PhD, he's just a carpenter's kid like us. Why does he think he can do this job of instructing *us* about God? His brothers are our homeboys and his sisters our homegirls; so, who does he think he is?

> *Mark 6:2-5 Amplified Version*
> *² And on the Sabbath He began to teach in the synagogue; and many who listened to Him were utterly astonished, saying, Where did this [a]Man acquire all this? What is the wisdom [the broad and full intelligence which has been] given to Him? What mighty works and exhibitions of power are wrought by His hands! ³ Is not this the Carpenter, the son of Mary and the brother of James and Joses and Judas and Simon? And are not His sisters here among us? And they took offense at Him and [b]were hurt [that is, they [c]disapproved of Him, and it hindered them from acknowledging His authority] and they were caused to stumble and fall. ⁴ But Jesus said to them, A prophet is not without honor (deference, reverence) except in his [own] country and among [his] relatives and in his [own] house. ⁵ And He was not able to do [d]even one work of power there, except that He laid His hands on a few sickly people [and] cured them.*

In Mark 6:2-5, their questions and reasoning reflected how they were stumbling in their minds, questioning His authority and offended that someone they grew up with could surpass them in wisdom, power, authority and understanding. It's as if they were saying, "How dare you become someone who broke these Narazene limits we have settled to be confined to all our lives?" The issue was not whether Jesus was qualified: it was their own hearts, their own complacency and their own lack of revelation. It seems unfathomable that God incarnate could be standing right in front of someone and he or she still rejects Him. If they could reject an overqualified Jesus, it lets us know that rejection is an indictment against them and their hardened hearts.

I often wonder how Jesus felt knowing that He would have to die for the very people who treated him with such disdain. It stands to reason that this is why the scripture instructs us to love our enemies—they have their own issues that only love can conquer.

Similarly, in 1 Samuel 8, the children of Israel reject Jehovah as king.

> *1 Samuel 8:7*
> *And the Lord said unto Samuel, Hearken unto the voice of the people in all that they say unto thee: for they have not rejected thee, but they have rejected me, that I should not reign over them.*

> *1 Samuel 10:19*
> *And ye have this day rejected your God, who himself saved you out of all your adversities and your tribulations; and ye have said unto him, Nay, but set a king over us. Now therefore present yourselves before the Lord by your tribes, and by your thousands.*

He had suffered with their stiffneckedness, their stubbornness and their rebellion in the wilderness. He brought them out of Egypt with a strong hand, He sent undeniable plagues and rescued them from the heavy hands of their oppressor and still--- because they saw other nations with kings—they wanted a human king to which they could point. You tell me, was the problem with God or with them? Was this a sign that there was something wrong with the rejecter or the one being rejected?

Consider an alternate view of rejection: it is a sign that those who are rejecting you don't have the capacity to receive you. Like those in Jesus' home town, they are stumbling and falling at the thought of you—not because you are unqualified but because your progress is an indictment to their apathy and complacency with their surroundings. Because all they can see is only what they have seen all their lives, you and your difference is a threat to them and therefore, they reject you.

Jesus gives us a great example of what to do in this circumstance—move on! Jesus healed a few sick people and then moved on to the surrounding villages. He didn't' stay in Nazareth and try to convince them that He was who He said He was. He just did what He had to do and moved on—and you should too!

Isn't it amazing how people who grew up in the same town, economic status, schools and roots as you somehow think they have something different going for them that justifies rejecting you? Too often, we judge people because of their backgrounds, because they don't yet have money or because they don't look like what we think they should look like. Thank God for His Word that declares that the "stone that the builders rejected became the chief corner stone."

Matthew 21:42

Jesus saith unto them, Did ye never read in the scriptures, The stone which the builders rejected, the same is become the head of the corner: this is the Lord's doing, and it is marvellous in our eyes?

Mark 12:10

And have ye not read this scripture; The stone which the builders rejected is become the head of the corner:

Luke 20:17

And he beheld them, and said, What is this then that is written, The stone which the builders rejected, the same is become the head of the corner?

The Message Bible says it this way:
Matthew 21:42

Jesus said, "Right—and you can read it for yourselves in your Bibles:

*The stone the masons threw out
   is now the cornerstone.
This is God's work;
   we rub our eyes, we can hardly believe it!*

These scriptures are a wonderful illustration of what rejection is and what God can do with those who have suffered rejection and betrayal. It likens the process of rejection to a construction worker getting together all of the materials he or she needs to build a house: plywood, bricks, nails, concrete, hammers, etc. While going through the bricks he notices one that isn't to his liking. On the outside, it looks inferior so he throws it out. Along comes Contractor Jesus and He picks up the very brick that the construction worker has thrown out. With it, Contractor Jesus builds a masterpiece! It surpasses even what the construction worker is able to do with seemingly perfect bricks. This is what God is able to do with us "rejected bricks." Glory be to God!

The life of Joseph, one of the best "rejected brick" stories in the Word, is another example that rejection is a reflection of the rejecter(s). In the same way that Jesus' wisdom and power caused the folks in this hometown to stumble, Joseph's brothers stumbled at his favor and his dreams.

Gen 37:3
Now Israel loved Joseph more than all his children, because he was the son of his old age: and he made him a coat of many colours.

Genesis 37:5
And Joseph dreamed a dream, and he told it his brethren: and they hated him yet the more.

Gen 37:11
And his brethren envied him; but his father observed the saying.

Gen 37:18 - 20
And when they saw him afar off, even before he came near unto them, they conspired against him to slay him. And they said one to another, Behold, this dreamer cometh. Come now therefore, and let us slay him, and cast him into some pit, and we will say, Some evil beast hath devoured him: and we shall see what will become of his dreams.

Yikes—watch out for dream killers disguised as brethren! Jesus! His own brothers were the dream-killing assignment in his life! Why couldn't they just be happy for their brother? Why were their hearts full of envy to the point that they wanted to kill him?

Interestingly enough, their hatred and envy was the result of their own feelings of rejection. They felt rejected by their father, Israel, because he favored Joseph. And when rejection comes from a parent, it is more detrimental than any other kind of rejection. Why? Parents are not your equal, so you can't lash out at them the way you would at others. Also, parents play a major role in your identify formation and they are who you look to for love.

Imagine how the rest of Israel's sons must have felt. He [Israel] never made the rest of his sons a fine coat or treated them like he treated the son of his old age. Moreover, Israel (Jacob) never hid his love for Rachel. His sons lived knowing that their mother (Leah) was never as favored as Joseph's mother. It was enough that they had to live under that show for years; now a spoiled brat was trying to Lord it over them--no way!

The resentment had built up over the years. Their bleeding wound of rejection festered to the point that it turned into envy and then, finally hatred and murder. It was only the voice of Reuben that caused them to sell him into slavery instead of killing him. In this case, as in so many, rejection gives birth to more rejection. Joseph's brothers felt rejected by Israel so they rejected him.

Police officers, investigators and other justice professionals understand that motive, i.e. rejection is often at the root of violent crimes. Joseph's brothers went from resentment to rejection to envy to conspiracy and finally, to murder. When others conspire against you, know that something about you; typically, your favor makes them feel rejected or inferior in some way. It's a reflection on them—not on you.

If only we could respond the way Jesus responded—Father forgive them for they know not what they do. Truly, even with the benefit of Joseph's dreams, his brothers had no idea what they were doing. They did not know that the little brother they were selling into to slavery would be the source of their own freedom 13 years later. For this reason, whenever you are suffering at the hands of rejecters please stop to consider if God is setting you up for perfection. What do I mean by that? Look at the words of Jesus and note what He calls perfection.

> *Mat 5:43-48*
> *Ye have heard that it hath been said, Thou shalt love thy neighbour, and hate thine enemy. But I say unto you, Love your enemies, bless them that curse you, do good to them that hate you, and pray for them which despitefully use you, and persecute you; That ye may be the children of your Father which is in heaven: for he maketh his sun to rise on the evil and on the good, and sendeth rain on the just and on the unjust. For if ye love them which love you, what reward have ye? do not even the publicans the same? And if ye salute your brethren only, what do ye more than others? do not even the publicans so? Be ye therefore perfect, even as your Father which is in heaven is perfect.*

What could be more perfect than loving someone who has rejected you? When we do this, we become little Jesus's, laying down our lives and forgiving the very people who persecute us. Over time, Joseph was able to do this as well; showing us that the only power that overcomes rejection is true, agape (unconditional) love.

Chapter Conclusion

The Israelites rejected God and, like other nations, wanted a human king. Residents of Jesus hometown stumbled at him, murmuring to themselves "is this not the carpenter's son?" And Joseph was rejected and betrayed by his own brothers because he was favored and had dreams. Each of these instances revealed the hearts of the rejecter(s) and pointed to their inadequacies— not to the one they were rejecting.

Rejection is a reflection of the rejecter's inability to love, their limited capacity to receive you or some other negative emotion (like envy) that they have not been able to break free from.

No matter who it is—parent, acquaintance or foe—being rejected doesn't mean there's anything wrong with you. Likely, it means something is right. Our perfect Father God and His dear son Jesus were rejected and you can't get more right than those two.

Perhaps your rejecter has his or her own issues to sort out. Would you be like Jesus and declare, "Father forgive them for they know not what they do?" Know that there's nothing wrong with you. There's a gift of God inside of you and you are more than what your rejecters say you are.

For maximum benefit, please answer the following questions in an individual journal and/or in a group discussion setting.

1.) Read 1 Samuel 8:1-7. For what reason did the elders of Israel want a king? Do you think their request was justified and why?
2.) How do you think their request made God feel? Why do you think God responded the way He did?
3.) Revisit Mark 6:2-5 and Mark 12:10. Why do you think the people in Jesus' home town rejected him? How is this a reflection on them?
4.) How did the role/actions of the parent, Joseph's father, impact Joseph's situation? What might you have done if you were one of Joseph's father? What might you have done if you were his brothers?
5.) Is there anything about Joseph's or Jesus' rejection that you find similar to your own experience? Explain.

Prayer

Heavenly Father, I give you thanks for the blood of Jesus that was shed for my redemption. I thank you that Jesus was willing to suffer rejection for my deliverance. Give me a heart of understanding and love that I might be able to love beyond the rejection.

I thank you for my rejecters and I understand that their rejection is not a reflection of me but them. Bring healing into their lives as you bring it into mine. I resist and cast out the spirit of rejection from my life and I receive your love. Thank you for understanding what rejection feels like. Thank you for sending Jesus to die for it. Amen.

Rejection is a Setup for Promotion

If you could put on special eyeglasses that allowed you to see life through someone else's eyes what might you learn? Consider life through Jesus' eyes just before the last nail went into his body on the cross. Now, imagine life through his eyes when he arose the third day after his crucifixion. Life must have looked, tasted and felt very different at those two moments.

What has life looked, tasted and smelled like during your moments of rejection? If rejection has a taste it is bitter, making it difficult to imagine that there is ever a taste of honey in the future. Jesus' advantage on the cross was that he knew that there was honey in his future so he endured the shame and rejection of the cross. He knew that he would eventually be glorified.

However, when you and I face rejection is it not always with a better end in mind. Still, it is useful to ask whether there can be something valuable in rejection. In the life of Jesus, it was a stepping stone—a setup—that allowed him to become the chief corner stone. Could it be the same in your life?

> *Luke 17:24-25*
> *²⁴ For as the lightning, that lighteneth out of the one part under heaven, shineth unto the other part under heaven; so shall also the Son of man be in his day. ²⁵ But first must he suffer many things, and be rejected of this generation.*

Jesus addressed the disciples in Luke 17:24-25 and painted a picture of his future. He told him that he would be like the lightning that comes from one side of heaven and shines upon people in another part of heaven. He also told them that he first had to be rejected by the current generation. His attitude towards rejection was that he had accepted it as an irrefutable part of his life and ministry. He was never taken by surprise by rejection—in fact, he always knew what was in the heart of men.

> *John 2:24-25*
> *24 But Jesus did not commit himself unto them, because he knew all men, 25 And needed not that any should testify of man: for he knew what was in man.*

What is to be learned from Jesus is not to expect rejection but rather, not to expect everyone to embrace you and/or your vision. Matthew Henry said it this way, "Jesus had to encounter a generation of unbelieving Jews to save believing Gentiles and had to go through the cross before receiving a crown." While there were those who did not embrace Jesus, there were also those who were *called to* receive him.

Similarly, you are called to a particular sphere of influence. There will be those who will reject you but this is simply an indication that they are not the ones called to receive you and/or your vision. *This is one positive aspect of rejection—it lets you know the people who are not called to support you and your vision. See this as a gift!*

Look for those who will support you and your vision—change friends if necessary; but let rejection serve you, as a compass directing you and redirecting you to those who will support and believe in what God has placed inside you.

Joseph's life demonstrates another positive aspect of rejection. From the pit, to Potiphar's house to prison to the palace, Joseph had to come to grips with a decision. That decision was whether to let betrayal and rejection keep him bitter or make him better, relying more fully on God. Undoubtedly, rejection has brought you or someone you know to this same decision. From this standpoint, rejection has the positive aspect of helping us rely more fully on God.

Not only did Joseph have to endure betrayal but it was the thing that God himself decided to use to get Joseph in position for his destiny. If Joseph had not been sold into slavery he would not have ended up in Egypt and would never have been in position to go to Potiphar's house. If he hadn't been betrayed by Potiphar's wife, he would not have gone to the prison. If he had not gone to the prison, he would not have interpreted the cupbearer's dream. If he had not interpreted the cupbearer's dream, he would never have gone before Pharaoh to interpret his dream and thus, would not have become the governor of Egypt. In each phase of Joseph's life, God used rejection as a stepping-stone to the next phase of Joseph's journey to the governorship.

Joseph's Life Stage	Betrayed by
Home/Family	Joseph's brothers
Potiphar's house	Potiphar's wife
Prison	Cup-bearer

David's words remind us that rejection is an opportunity to rely more fully on God:

> *Psalm 27:10*
> *When my father and my mother forsake me, then the Lord will take me up.*

Only by relying on God can you choose to forgive, move on and keep pursuing purpose in the face of betrayal and rejection. David reminds us that even when the people closest to us and expected to love us the most reject us, the Lord will take us up. Those are actually the defining moments of your life. The make or break moments in which you either turn to God and let the situation make you better or continue to hold on to negative emotions and be crippled by bitterness, anger and unforgiveness.

Our response to rejection determines our readiness for promotion. When we turn to God, he can exalt us and promote us and he has an opportunity to become our defender and shield. If, instead, you hold on to negative emotions and become bitter, God first has to deal with the issues of your own heart. Deciding to let rejection make us better hastens the healing and promotion process.

It is so wonderful to see the results of Joseph's decision to let go as evidenced in the blessing that his father, Israel, pronounced upon him before he died.

> *Deuteronomy 33:16-17*
> *16 And for the precious things of the earth and fulness thereof, and for the good will of him that dwelt in the bush: let the blessing come upon the head of Joseph, and upon the top of the head of him that was separated from his brethren. 17 His glory is like the firstling of his bullock, and his horns are like the horns of unicorns: with them he shall push the people together to the ends of the earth: and they are the ten thousands of Ephraim, and they are the thousands of Manasseh.*

In the same way that Jesus' decision to endure the shame of the cross resulted in a crown of glory so did Joseph's decision to let rejection and betrayal make him better—instead of bitter.

Genesis 29:31
And when the Lord saw that Leah was hated, he opened her womb...

The life of Leah is yet another—and one of the greatest—example of the possible turnaround that can come from rejection. In this instance, God himself reacts to Leah's rejection. Leah was the oldest daughter of Laban, Jacob's uncle. Jacob, the trickster had traveled to his uncle's hometown in search of refuge from his angry brother Esau. Jacob feared that Esau was in pursuit of him because he [Jacob], under the advisement of his mother, had cheated Esau out of his birthright. When Jacob arrives at Laban's hometown he immediately fell in love with Rachel, Laban's younger daughter. However, it was the custom of Laban's people that the oldest must marry before the younger. Laban tricks Jacob, putting Leah in his bed (instead of Rachel) on the night that he was supposed to consummate his marriage to Rachel.

Jacob never hid is his love for Rachel even after being tricked into marrying Leah. The scripture never expounds on Leah's point of view but imagine how she must have felt. She was outshined by her little sister, unloved and stuck in a marriage that we don't' even know that she ever wanted. Leah was in a situation that may be one of the most miserable states of being in the world—she was married but hated. What a horrible existence.

But what's more amazing is how God Himself responds to the situation.

> *Genesis 29:31a*
> *And when the Lord saw that Leah was hated, he opened her womb...*

How awesome! God turned Leah's rejection into a place and point of contact for conception. This is another positive aspect of rejection—it often causes you to do or try something different, to seek God for another way out and/or for clarity and refinement of vision. Rejection is actually the conception place or womb of vision.

So when you, your work, your ideas, your ministry or your creativity are rejected, re-evaluate your vision. Enhance it. Refine it. Rework it. And move on to the next potential supporter. The ones who rejected you will have actually made your vision stronger and better. Don't retaliate against your rejecters. Rather, cry out to the Lord asking Him to open the womb of vision in your life to a greater measure.

Remember, when the Lord Jesus was rejected He didn't retaliate.

Isaiah 53:7
He was oppressed, and he was afflicted, yet he opened
not his mouth

When God sees that you are willing to stay humble and work through the rejection He in turn will exalt you.

Chapter Conclusion

Physical wounds sometimes leave scars, which can serve as reminders to us to use caution and/or to proceed differently. Similarly, there are some positive outcomes that can be derived from rejection. For Jesus, it was a stepping-stone to His seat at the right hand of Father. For Joseph, it repeatedly propelled him into divine purpose and for Leah; God opened her womb and gave her the precious gift of a son. In each case, the key of rejection being a springboard was in their response to it. How will you respond?

Decide that rejection will make you better and not bitter. Let rejection drive you back into a place of crying out to God for greater clarity of vision and don't' retaliate. As Jesus did, love those who reject you and move on (metaphorically or physically if needed) to other towns where you will find the support you need.

Reflection questions:

For maximum benefit, please answer the following questions in an individual journal and/or in a group discussion setting.

1.) Do you agree that there can be valuable benefits derived from rejection and why? Discuss how positive outcomes may actually result from rejection.
2.) Reflect on your experiences with rejection. Were there any positive outcomes and if so, what were they?

3.) How can we cultivate the attitude that Jesus had towards rejection in Luke 17:24-25?

4.) Why do you think God opened Leah's womb? Has God intervened in your life in this way yet? If so, how?

Prayer

Heavenly Father, thank you for the examples of Jesus, Joseph and Leah. Whatever rejection I am experiencing now or have experienced, I lay it before you and ask that, by your grace, it would make me better and not bitter. Open the womb of my spirit with vision; vision that allows me to see myself as you see me; vision that opens my eyes to what you have called me to do; vision that open my eyes to the possibilities ahead of me and to those who have the capacity to embrace me. I pray in Jesus name, Amen.

Untreated Rejection Causes Festering Wounds

Infected wounds stink with the smell of rotting, decaying flesh. If you've ever had a major surgical incision such as a cesarean incision or vasectomy, you understand how important it is to keep such cuts clean and dry. Similarly, if left untreated, rejection's emotional wounds and cuts bleed, stink and fester in the soul, creating damaging side-effects that are more detrimental than rejection itself.

In the natural, people with infected wounds have a heightened sensitivity to touch in the area of their wound(s). Similarly, when people are wounded from rejection, they can develop a heightened sensitivity in their souls; becoming overly defensive, unable to handle criticism, prone to self-pity and easily angered. These ill effects are an increased incentive for us to decide that rejection will make us better not bitter. How we respond to rejection makes a difference in our own ability to avoid rejection's negative side effects. The account of Cain and Abel illustrates some of these damaging side-effects.

> *Genesis 4:2-5 (New King James Version)*
> *Then she bore again, this time his brother Abel. Now Abel was a keeper of sheep, but Cain was a tiller of the ground. ³ And in the process of time it came to pass that Cain brought an offering of the fruit of the ground to the LORD. ⁴ Abel also brought of the firstborn of his flock and of their fat. And the LORD respected Abel and his offering, ⁵ but He did not respect Cain and his offering. And Cain was very angry, and his countenance fell.*

When Cain's offering did not receive God's approval his countenance fell; the New Living Translation says he looked "dejected." Perhaps he felt outdone by his little brother. He felt dejected or downcast, despondent or disheartened. God had rejected his offering—but not him. Sadly, Cain could not separate those two things. As a result, Cain became very angry, jealous, envious, and eventually committed murder.

> *Genesis 4:5-8 (New International Version)*
> …but on Cain and his offering he did not look with favor. So Cain was very angry, and his face was downcast. ⁶ Then the LORD said to Cain, "Why are you angry? Why is your face downcast? ⁷ If you do what is right, will you not be accepted? But if you do not do what is right, sin is crouching at your door; it desires to have you, but you must rule over it." ⁸ Now Cain said to his brother Abel, "Let's go out to the field." While they were in the field, Cain attacked his brother Abel and killed him.

How rejection's side effects are handled is very important. Cain couldn't properly deal with the anger he felt and, as a result ended up murdering his own brother. Sibling rivalries and family dysfunction are often the result of poorly handled feelings of rejection. The account of Cain and Abel reveals rejection's side effects of anger, jealousy and murder.

According to Webster, anger is an intense emotional state induced by displeasure. It is important to note that it is defined as a "state." This implies that it is a place (state or locale) that God never intended man to reside or remain. It is not a permanent residence but rather an occasional visiting place. If mismanaged, it opens the door to varying levels of manifestation like ire, rage, fury, indignation, and wrath. It is important to note the characteristics of each level of anger:

1.   Anger, the most general term, names the reaction but in itself conveys nothing about intensity or justification or manifestation of the emotional state. There is not necessarily an evident display of feelings.

2. Ire, more frequent in literary contexts, may suggest greater intensity than anger, often with an evident display of feeling.
3. Rage suggests loss of self-control from violence of emotion. Clamor is associated with rage.
4. Fury is overmastering destructive rage that can verge on madness.
5. Indignation stresses righteous anger at what one considers unfair, mean, or shameful.
6. Wrath is likely to suggest a desire or intent to revenge or punish. Wrath is the kind of anger that leads to murder.

By implication, Cain's anger against his brother had reached a level of wrath. In his wrath and desire for vengeance, he murdered his own brother. The various manifestations listed above are all a result of mismanaged anger and wrong reactions to rejection. If not dealt with at level one, anger will escalate and become wrath. Perhaps if Cain had taken steps to deal with his anger, he would not have killed his brother. Each person must ask herself/himself, how am I handling rejection? Is it making me bitter or making me better? Have I made a conscious decision to release and forgive those who have rejected me or am I holding on to resentment and anger?

David took the attitude that "I will not touch the Lord's anointed." In light of the fact that Saul had tried to kill him, David's attitude is a challenge and an example to anyone who has been rejected and/or betrayed. David had every right to be angry with Saul. Not only had he tried to kill David but he was sitting on a throne that no longer belonged to him—a throne for which David had been anointed. Still, David was convicted in his heart not to do any harm to Saul.

And it came to pass afterward, that David's heart smote him, because he had cut off Saul's skirt. [6] And he said unto his men, The LORD forbid that I should do this thing unto my master, the LORD's anointed, to stretch forth mine hand

against him, seeing he is the anointed of the LORD. ⁷ So David
stayed his servants with these words, and suffered them not
to rise against Saul. But Saul rose up out of the cave, and
went on his way. – 1 Samuel 24:5-7 (King James Version)

Our response to rejection is a matter of the heart. When faced
with rejection and betrayal the best thing you can do is cry out to
God to keep your heart pure and give you the strength to forgive.
Some of the greatest psalms of David were birthed out of his
being rejected and betrayed. David sang the words of Psalms 18
after God delivered him from the hand of all his enemies and the
hand of Saul. He [David] said:

Psalm 18: 16-21 (New Living Translation)
He reached down from heaven and rescued me; He drew me
out of deep waters. He rescued me from my powerful
enemies, from those who hated me and were too strong for
me. They attached me at a moment when I was in distress,
but the Lord supported me. He led me to a place of safety; he
rescued me because he delights in me. The Lord rewarded
me for doing right; he restored me for because of my
innocence. For I have kept the ways of the Lord; I have not
turned from my God to follow evil.

David could sing that he had kept the ways of the Lord because
he did not harm Saul. Perhaps if Cain had responded this way
God could have vindicated him as well. Instead, Cain slew his
brother.

Saul was rejected from being king by God Himself (due to his
own disobedience) and like Cain, also fell prey to rejection's
dangerous side effects of envy, jealousy, hatred and murder:

1 Samuel 18:7-11 (KJV)
And the women answered one another as they played,
and said, Saul hath slain his thousands, and David his
ten thousands. And Saul was very wroth, and the saying
displeased him; and he said, They have ascribed unto

David ten thousands, and to me they have ascribed but thousands: and what can he have more but the kingdom? And Saul eyed [literally meaning that he looked with jealousy upon] David from that day and forward. And it came to pass on the morrow [the next day], that the evil spirit from God came upon Saul, and he prophesied in the midst of the house: and David played with his hand, as at other times: and there was a javelin in Saul's hand. And Saul cast the javelin; for he said, I will smite David even to the wall with it. And David avoided out of his presence twice.

First, in this passage, we see the women praising David for slaying his ten thousands, but Saul for slaying his thousands. This comparison made Saul angry with David, and envious of his success. Although often thought to be the same thing as jealousy, envy is defined as a feeling of discontent or covetousness with regard to another's advantages, success, possessions, etc. Rejoicing with others is a sign of maturity and taking their success as an indication that God can also bless you is an attitude that prevents the damaging side effects of rejection.

The very next day, an evil spirit came upon Saul and caused him to become exceedingly angry, to the point of attempting to murder David! This spirit was probably a spirit of envy or wrath. Now there's some ugly fruit! And it all started with Saul's response to rejection. It wasn't rejection that opened Saul up to the evil spirit, but rather his reaction to his rejection as king and comparison to David.

The same is true when a person becomes stubborn or rebellious, or any other ungodly reaction to rejection. The rejection isn't the sin, but their reaction can be a serious sin. This can open the person up to unclean spirits, and lead them down the path of destruction. God's Word puts stubbornness and rebellion, for example, in the same category as witchcraft and idol worship!

1 Samuel 15:23 (King James Version)
For rebellion is as the sin of witchcraft, and stubbornness
is as iniquity and idolatry. Because thou hast rejected the
word of the LORD, he hath also rejected thee from being
king.

Through the lives of Cain and Saul, it is evident that rejection, left unresolved or mismanaged, can result in:

- Anger
- Bitterness
- Resentment
- Self-pity
- Unforgiveness
- Pride
- Retaliation
- Envy
- Jealousy
- Hatred
- Murder

None of these spirits is your destiny. Numbers 5:14 and verse 30 tells us that jealousy is a spirit. Rejection opened the door for other spirits and they influenced Cain to murder his brother. It is time to clean any wounds that may be in your soul so that any side effects are driven out.

Chapter Conclusion

Take a self-inventory. Are there any side effects of rejection's wound that you need to clean? Are you able to pray for those who rejected you? Are you able to love them and embrace them? If not, this may be an indication of anger, bitterness, unforgiveness, resentment or pride. Are you able to rejoice with others who have what you wanted? If not, this may be an indication of envy or jealousy.

You may be able to mask your true feelings from others but you cannot mask them with God. He can create in us a clean heart and renew a right spirit within us just as he did for David. Saul's actions were not right and were not justified but David did not use that as an excuse to stray from the Lord's ways. Decide that rejection will make you better and not bitter. Let rejection drive you back into a place of crying out to God for a clean heart and don't retaliate. As David did, continue to walk with an upright heart toward God and toward those who reject you. Then, as David learned, God can reward you.

Reflection questions:

For maximum benefit, please answer the following questions in an individual journal and/or in a group discussion setting.

1.) Are there any side effects of rejection that you find particularly difficult to handle and why? Discuss and/or identify scriptures related to this side effect. See Chapter 7 for scriptures.
2.) If Cain had later brought a better sacrifice, would God have accepted it? Why?
3.) What was it that kept David from harming Saul? What caused him to restrain himself? How can you apply this in your life?

Prayer

Heavenly Father, thank you for the example of David, who when betrayed would not harm Saul, his betrayer. Give me the strength to walk uprightly with you and with those who have rejected me as David did. Forgive me for any side effect of rejection that I have allowed to persist in my life. I renounce anger, pride, envy, jealousy, hatred and any other side effect in my life. I ask you to create in me a clean heart and renew a right spirit within me. In Jesus name, Amen.

God Heals Rejection and its Wounds and Restores Self-Concept

Psalm 147:2-3
2 The Lord doth build up Jerusalem: he gathereth together the outcasts of Israel.3 He healeth the broken in heart, and bindeth up their wounds

Jeremiah 30:17
For I will restore health unto thee, and I will heal thee of thy wounds, saith the Lord; because they called thee an Outcast, saying, This is Zion, whom no man seeketh after.

After conception, the Lord hides us in the waters of our mother's womb for months. Before that moment ever takes place, He has already mapped out our purpose and recorded each day of our lives in His book (Psalm 139:16). When you enter this world, you are already endowed with purpose. It's on the inside of you concealed in the wrapping paper of human flesh and revealed more and more as you grow in your relationship with the Lord. Our lives are hidden in Christ; or, in other words, our purpose is encoded in the DNA of Jesus on the inside of us—eternity in our hearts. The more we awaken to the DNA of Jesus, the more we awaken to our purpose. What better tool then, of the enemy, than to use rejection to rob us of the realization of our true selves—to rob us of revelation of what I call, our "Jesus DNA."

Remember, rejection is carried out by a spirit and the rejection you have experienced in the past or are experiencing has four primary, specific purposes; namely, to cripple:

1. Your ability to know God intimately as a loving Father
2. Your belief in and understanding of your true identify— your Jesus DNA
3. Your ability to know and love others

4. Others' ability to receive God's message through you

God heals us from rejection from the inside out. He heals the wounds and infections (side effects) in our soul and He also gives us a vision of our true selves. Through His word and, relationship with Him through Jesus Christ, He restores and repairs our self-concept, identity and esteem.

Self-concept is a global understanding of yourself. It shapes and defines who you are, the decisions you make and the relationships you form. It is perhaps, the basis for all motivated behavior[3]. It involves the sense of being separate and distinct from others and the awareness of the constancy of the self".[4]

One of the first aspects of a godly self-concept is an awareness that you, as an individual originated from the Father [God]. The word father actually means source[5]: you originated in the mind of your Heavenly Father and you have His nature and DNA in you. You were not a mistake but were carefully fashioned or, in other words, designed by God. Understanding and believing this at a deep level forms a solid foundation for a healthy self-concept. When you believe and understand this, you know without a doubt that you are God's masterpiece—His workmanship. You existed in the mind of God the Father before you were formed in your mother's womb and you will exist after your earthly body ceases.

> *Ephesians 2:10 (New Living Translation)*
> *For we are God's masterpiece. He has created us anew in Christ Jesus, so we can do the good things he planned for us long ago.*

---

[3] Franken, 1994,
http://assets.cengage.com/pdf/smp_4713_chapter%2015.pdf
[4] Bee, 1992, http://assets.cengage.com/pdf/smp_4713_chapter%2015.pdf
[5] http://www.biblewheel.com/Wheel/Spokes/Aleph_GodTheFather.php

Meditate on that scripture for a moment. It means that in the same way that a painter takes a brush and applies strokes of paint to create a masterpiece, God also designed you. He was first inspired (in His mind), just as an artist receives inspiration. He was creative and He had a particular purpose in mind when He fashioned/designed you as His masterpiece.

When an artist creates something they deem a masterpiece, they dote over it, they admire their own work, they show it off and they treasure it. This is God's attitude toward you. If self-concept involves the sense of being separate and distinct from others and the awareness of the constancy of the self, the implications of Ephesians 2:10 for your self-concept are:

- You came from God and will end with God; He is your life source
- You were created by God as a masterpiece
- You were uniquely designed; you are not like others
- God had a unique intent in mind when He designed you—you have a divine purpose

Oh that you would believe this like never before and replace rejection thinking with "God DNA" thinking. Your self-concept should be that you are an original masterpiece. You originated in the mind of God and were designed, fashioned and formed by Him with a unique purpose. There is no one else on earth like you—no other fingerprint exactly like yours. That is the design of God. From now on, let your self-concept be a "masterpiece" self-concept.

Not only does God give us a proper self-concept but He also demonstrated our worth, our value and our esteem by sacrificing His only son on a bloody cross for you and me. Romans 5:8 says, "But God demonstrates His own love toward us, in that while we were still sinners, Christ died for us." (New King James Version) The Father put His love in action, placed value on you and wasn't afraid to show it. The scripture goes on to say that you have great value.

Luke 12:24 (The Living Bible)
²⁴ Look at the ravens—they don't plant or harvest or have barns to store away their food, and yet they get along all right—for God feeds them. And *you are far more valuable to him than any birds*!

Understanding how much value God has placed upon you has a direct link to your self-esteem:

> People with poor self-esteem often rely on how they are doing in the present to determine how they feel about themselves. They need positive external experiences (e.g., compliments from friends) to counteract the negative feelings and thoughts that constantly plague them. Even then, the good feeling (such as from a good grade or compliment) is usually temporary.
>
> Healthy self-esteem is based on our ability to assess ourselves accurately and still be accepting of who we are. This means being able to acknowledge our strengths and weaknesses (we all have them) and at the same time recognize that we are worthy and worthwhile. [6]

Jesus has already told you that you are valuable to Him and the Father. He goes on to say, "he has made us accepted in the beloved." (Ephesians 1:6) He already knows your thoughts afar off, your sitting down, rising up and your strengths and weaknesses; yet, He still accepts you. Even as the scripture says, He will never leave your or forsake you (Hebrews 13:5). You don't have to worry about His acceptance. He already knows you are not perfect but still places great value on you. If the *precious*, blood of Jesus is worthwhile and of value, then so are you because it was shed for you. So, whether you make a mistake or not, God's value on your life doesn't change. He still calls you accepted and still shed the precious blood of Jesus for you. Let

[6] http://cmhc.utexas.edu/selfesteem.html

your self-esteem be in that and, in the fact that He calls you a son or a daughter.

Not only does God heal our self-concept and restore our self-esteem but also gives us a true sense of identity. Self-identity is the recognition of one's potential and qualities as an individual.[7] Not only does God design and fashion you as a masterpiece, sacrifice the precious blood of His own son for you but then goes on to endow you with gifts, abilities and talents (qualities and potential) so that you can do greater works than even Jesus did when He was on earth:

> John 14:12 (King James Version)
> Verily, verily, I say unto you, He that believeth on me, the works that I do shall he do also; and greater works than these shall he do; because I go unto my Father.

You are loaded with potential! You have talents, gifts and abilities that came from the Father! Perhaps you have yet to discover them or may have discovered them and still need to hone or sharpen them, but God has given you something and He expects that you will use it for His glory and in the process, for your own fulfillment. He has called you and in that calling is your identity. In the natural, children take their identity from their fathers. That is why children carry the last name of their fathers. You, as a son or daughter of God, take your identify from your heavenly father. He has decided what qualities and unique abilities you need to fulfill your purpose. The more you discover your purpose, the more you discover your identity.

Jesus endured rejection so that you and I can be free from rejection. The enemy's weapon of rejection is therefore another illegal weapon because all your feelings of rejection are now covered under the blood of Jesus.

---

[7] Google.com

If you don't fully exercise the power of the blood of Jesus, infections can spread from the wounds in your souls. It is time for all of these things to be broken off your life—reject the rejecter. Jesus was rejected so that you and I can be free from rejection. Re-examine the following prophetic portion of scripture concerning Jesus' obedience to the Cross:

> *He is despised and rejected of men; a man of sorrows, and acquainted with grief: and we hid as it were our faces from him; he was despised, and we esteemed him not. Surely he hath borne our griefs, and carried our sorrows: yet we did esteem him stricken, smitten of God, and afflicted. But he was wounded for our transgressions, he was bruised for our iniquities: the chastisement of our peace was upon him; and with his stripes we are healed. – Isaiah 53:3-5 (King James Version)*

Give the enemy back his rejection—Jesus paid the price for yours when He died on the Cross. God declares that you are accepted in the beloved, fearfully and wonderfully made, the apple of His eye, a royal priest, an excellent one, above only, the head, blessed, highly favored, called, chosen, loved, overcoming, conquering, victorious, triumphant, and more. There's no need for you to feel rejected by anyone because everyone has one issue of their own or another.

The enemy always seeks to kill, steal, and destroy. God seeks to bring life. Consider Merriam Webster's definition of rejection:

- to refuse to accept, consider, submit to, take for some purpose, or use
- to refuse to hear, receive, or admit : rebuff, repel
- to refuse as lover or spouse
- to cast off
- throw back, repulse, to spew out

In contrast, God:

- Accepts us and give us purpose (Ephesians 1:6)
- Hears our cry and attends unto our speech (Psalm 18:6)
- Is the lover of our souls (Jeremiah 31:3)
- Takes us under the shadow of His wings (Psalm 57:1)
- Calls us unto Himself (2 Timothy 1:9)
- Embraces us (Song of Solomon 2:6)

Chapter Conclusion

God is love (1 John 4:8). The very essence of His nature is the antithesis of the spirit of rejection. Never allow the enemy to make you join his rejection club. He was the one that was rejected and cast out of heaven because he rose up in pride declaring that he would be like God (Isaiah 14:13). Because he has lost his relationship with the Father (Luke 10:18), he wants to destroy yours through rejection. Take to heart the "God DNA" self-concept, knowing that you are His masterpiece. You don't have to place your self-esteem/self-worth in doing good deeds or never missing the mark. Paul was convinced that there is nothing that can separate you and I from the love of God and so am I (Romans 8:39).

Reflection questions:

For maximum benefit, please answer the following questions in an individual journal and/or in a group discussion setting.

1.) Discuss the "God DNA"/masterpiece self-concept. What does it mean to you and how can you apply it to your life?
2.) In what ways did God demonstrate our worth/esteem?
3.) How does God's character and demonstration of love differ from the definition of rejection?

Heavenly Father, I confess that rejection has bruised my soul. You are my Father and according to your Word, I am accepted in the beloved. I renounce the spirit of rejection. I ask that you heal my soul from the inner bruises of rejection. I give the devil back his illegal weapons of rejection and I declare that they are nailed to the Cross and washed away by the blood of Jesus. I renew my mind with your "God DNA" self-concept. Let your love wash over my soul and cleanse all the bruises from within. In Jesus name, I pray. Amen.

Scriptures Related to Rejection's Side Effects

Anger

Proverbs 14:16,17 A wise man feareth, and departeth from evil: but the fool rageth, and is confident. He that is soon angry dealeth foolishly: and a man of wicked devices is hated.

Proverbs 14:29 Whoever is slow to anger has great understanding, but he who has a hasty temper exalts folly.

Proverbs 19:11 Good sense makes one slow to anger, and it is his glory to overlook an offense.

Ecclesiastes 7:9 Be not quick in your spirit to become angry, for anger lodges in the bosom of fools.

James 1:19,20 Know this, my beloved brothers: let every person be quick to hear, slow to speak, slow to anger; for the anger of man does not produce the righteousness of God.

Matthew 5:21-24 "You have heard that it was said to those of old, 'You shall not murder; and whoever murders will be liable to judgment.' But I say to you that everyone who is angry with his brother will be liable to judgment; whoever insults his brother will be liable to the council; and whoever says, 'You fool!' will be liable to the hell of fire. So if you are offering your gift at the altar and there remember that your brother has something against you, leave your gift there before the altar and go. First be reconciled to your brother, and then come and offer your gift..." (Jesus' words)

Galatians 5:19-21 Now the works of the flesh are evident: sexual immorality, impurity, sensuality, idolatry, sorcery, enmity, strife, jealousy, fits of anger, rivalries, dissensions, divisions, envy, drunkenness, orgies, and things like these. I warn you, as I warned you before, that those who do such things will not inherit the kingdom of God.

Galatians 5:22-25 But the fruit of the Spirit is love, joy, peace, patience, kindness, goodness, faithfulness, gentleness, self-control; against such things there is no law. And those who belong to Christ Jesus have crucified the flesh with its passions and desires. If we live by the Spirit, let us also walk by the Spirit.

Ephesians 4:26-28 Be angry and do not sin; do not let the sun go down on your anger, and give no opportunity to the devil. Let the thief no longer steal, but rather let him labor, doing honest work with his own hands, so that he may have something to share with anyone in need.

Colossians 3:8, 12-13 But now you must put them all away: anger, wrath, malice, slander, and obscene talk from your mouth. Put on then, as God's chosen ones, holy and beloved, compassionate hearts, kindness, humility, meekness, and patience, bearing with one another and, if one has a complaint against another, forgiving each other; as the Lord has forgiven you, so you also must forgive.

Psalms 37:8 Refrain from anger, and forsake wrath! Fret not yourself; it tends only to evil.

Proverbs 15:18 A hot-tempered man stirs up strife, but he who is slow to anger quiets contention.

Proverbs 29:22 A man of wrath stirs up strife, and one given to anger causes much transgression.

Proverbs 30:33 For pressing milk produces curds, pressing the nose produces blood, and pressing anger produces strife.

Bitterness/Resentment

Job 21:25 And another dies in the bitterness of his soul, and never eats with pleasure.

Job 23:2 Even to day is my complaint bitter: my stroke is heavier than my groaning.

Psalms 71:20 You, which have showed me great and sore troubles, shall quicken me again, and shall bring me up again from the depths of the earth.

Proverbs 14:10 The heart knows his own bitterness; and a stranger does not intermeddle with his joy.

Proverbs 17:25 A foolish son is a grief to his father, and bitterness to her that bore him.

Ephesians 4:31 Let all bitterness, and wrath, and anger, and clamor, and evil speaking, be put away from you, with all malice:

James 3:14 But if you have bitter envying and strife in your hearts, glory not, and lie not against the truth.

1 John 2:9 He that said he is in the light, and hates his brother, is in darkness even until now.

Proverbs 20: 22 ESV
Do not say, "I will repay evil"; wait for the Lord, and he will deliver you.

Hebrews 12:14-15 ESV
Strive for peace with everyone, and for the holiness without which no one will see the Lord. See to it that no one fails to obtain the grace of God; that no "root of bitterness" springs up and causes trouble, and by it many become defiled;

Self-pity

1 Thessalonians 5:18 ESV Give thanks in all circumstances; for this is the will of God in Christ Jesus for you.

James 1:1-27 ESV James, a servant of God and of the Lord Jesus Christ, To the twelve tribes in the Dispersion: Greetings. Count it all joy, my brothers, when you meet trials of various kinds, for you know that the testing of your faith produces steadfastness. And let steadfastness have its full effect, that you may be perfect and complete, lacking in nothing. If any of you lacks wisdom, let him ask God, who gives generously to all without reproach, and it will be given him....

James 5:13 ESV Is anyone among you suffering? Let him pray. Is anyone cheerful? Let him sing praise.

Hebrews 13:5 ESV Keep your life free from love of money, and be content with what you have, for he has said, "I will never leave you nor forsake you."

Psalm 51:12 ESV Restore to me the joy of your salvation, and uphold me with a willing spirit.

Philippians 4:13 ESV I can do all things through him who strengthens me.

James 5:11 ESV Behold, we consider those blessed who remained steadfast. You have heard of the steadfastness of Job, and you have seen the purpose of the Lord, how the Lord is compassionate and merciful.

1 Peter 1:13 ESV Therefore, preparing your minds for action, and being sober-minded, set your hope fully on the grace that will be brought to you at the revelation of Jesus Christ.

Matthew 16:24-25 ESV Then Jesus told his disciples, "If anyone would come after me, let him deny himself and take up his cross and follow me. For whoever would save his life will lose it, but whoever loses his life for my sake will find it.

Psalm 135:14 ESV For the Lord will vindicate his people and have compassion on his servants.

Ephesians 2:8 ESV For by grace you have been saved through faith. And this is not your own doing; it is the gift of God,

Unforgiveness

Matthew 6: 14 For if you forgive people their trespasses [their reckless and willful sins, leaving them, letting them go, and giving up resentment], your heavenly Father will also forgive you.

Matthew 18: 21-22 Then Peter came up to Him and said, Lord, how many times may my brother sin against me and I forgive him and let it go? [As many as] up to seven times? Jesus answered him, I tell you, not up to seven times, but seventy times seven!

Matthew 18: 35 So also My heavenly Father will deal with every one of you if you do not freely forgive your brother from your heart his offenses.

Hebrews 8: 12 For I will be merciful and gracious toward their sins and I will remember their deeds of unrighteousness no more.

Colossians 3: 13 Be gentle and forbearing with one another and, if one has a difference (a grievance or complaint) against another, readily pardoning each other; even as the Lord has [freely] forgiven you, so must you also [forgive].

Psalm 86: 5 For You, O Lord, are good, and ready to forgive [our trespasses, sending them away, letting them go completely and forever]; and You are abundant in mercy and loving-kindness to all those who call upon You.

Mark 11:25 And whenever you stand praying, if you have anything against anyone, forgive him and let it drop (leave it, let it go), in order that your Father Who is in heaven may also forgive you your [own] failings and shortcomings and let them drop.

Ephesians 4:31-32 Let all bitterness and wrath and anger and clamor and slander be put away from you, along with all malice. Be kind to one another, tenderhearted, forgiving one another, as God in Christ forgave you. (attitude: loving and forgiving just like God forgave you)

1 Corinthians 13:4-7 Love is patient and kind; love does not envy or boast; it is not arrogant or rude. It does not insist on its own way; it is not irritable or resentful; it does not rejoice at wrongdoing, but rejoices with the truth. Love bears all things, believes all things, hopes all things, endures all things. (attitude: can love cover it?)

Matthew 5:44 But I tell you: Love your enemies and pray for those who persecute you,

Matthew 5:45 That you may be sons of your Father in heaven. He causes his sun to rise on the evil and the good, and sends rain on the righteous and the unrighteous.

Matthew 6:14 - For if you forgive men when they sin against you, your heavenly Father will also forgive you.

Mark 11:25 - And when you stand praying, if you hold anything against anyone, forgive him, so that your Father in heaven may forgive you your sins.

Romans 12:20 - On the contrary: "If your enemy is hungry, feed him, if he is thirsty, give him something to drink. In doing this, you will heap burning coals on his head.

Luke 6:35 - But love your enemies, do good to them, and lend to them without expecting to get anything back. Then your reward will be great, and you will be sons of the Most High, because he is kind to the ungrateful and wicked.

Luke 6:36 - Be merciful, just as your Father is merciful.

Luke 6:37 - "Do not judge, and you will not be judged. Do not condemn, and you will not be condemned.

Luke 6:38 - Give, and it will be given to you. A good measure, pressed down, shaken together and running over, will be poured into your lap. For with the measure you use, it will be measured to you."

Proverb 20:22 - Do not say, "I'll pay you back for this wrong!" Wait for the Lord, and he will deliver you.

Pride

Proverbs 16:5 - Every one [that is] proud in heart [is] an abomination to the LORD: [though] hand [join] in hand, he shall not be unpunished.

Proverbs 29:23 - A man's pride shall bring him low: but honour shall uphold the humble in spirit.

Galatians 6:3 - For if a man think himself to be something, when he is nothing, he deceiveth himself.

Proverbs 11:2 - [When] pride cometh, then cometh shame: but with the lowly [is] wisdom.

Proverbs 26:12 - Seest thou a man wise in his own conceit? [there is] more hope of a fool than of him.

James 4:6 - But he giveth more grace. Wherefore he saith, God resisteth the proud, but giveth grace unto the humble.

Proverbs 16:18 - Pride [goeth] before destruction, and an haughty spirit before a fall.

Proverbs 27:2 - Let another man praise thee, and not thine own mouth; a stranger, and not thine own lips.

1 John 2:16 - For all that [is] in the world, the lust of the flesh, and the lust of the eyes, and the pride of life, is not of the Father, but is of the world.

1 Peter 5:5 - Likewise, ye younger, submit yourselves unto the elder. Yea, all [of you] be subject one to another, and be clothed with humility: for God resisteth the proud, and giveth grace to the humble.

Philippians 2:3 - [Let] nothing [be done] through strife or vainglory; but in lowliness of mind let each esteem other better than themselves.

2 Timothy 3:2 - For men shall be lovers of their own selves, covetous, boasters, proud, blasphemers, disobedient to parents, unthankful, unholy,

Proverbs 25:27 - [It is] not good to eat much honey: so [for men] to search their own glory [is not] glory.

2 Corinthians 12:7 - And lest I should be exalted above measure through the abundance of the revelations, there was given to me a thorn in the flesh, the messenger of Satan to buffet me, lest I should be exalted above measure.

2 Corinthians 10:12 - For we dare not make ourselves of the number, or compare ourselves with some that commend themselves: but they measuring themselves by themselves, and comparing themselves among themselves, are not wise.

Romans 12:16 - [Be] of the same mind one toward another. Mind not high things, but condescend to men of low estate. Be not wise in your own conceits.

Retaliation

Romans 12:19 Never take your own revenge, beloved, but leave room for the wrath of God, for it is written, "Vengeance is mine I will repay," says the Lord.

Genesis 4:15 So the LORD said to him, "Therefore whoever kills Cain, vengeance will be taken on him sevenfold " And the

LORD appointed a sign for Cain, so that no one finding him would slay him.

Leviticus 19:18 'You shall not take vengeance, nor bear any grudge against the sons of your people, but you shall love your neighbor as yourself; I am the LORD.

Deuteronomy 32:35 'Vengeance is Mine, and retribution, In due time their foot will slip; For the day of their calamity is near, And the impending things are hastening upon them.'

Proverbs 20:22 Do not say, "I will repay evil"; Wait for the LORD, and He will save you.

Deuteronomy 19:5-7 as when a man goes into the forest with his friend to cut wood, and his hand swings the axe to cut down the tree, and the iron head slips off the handle and strikes his friend so that he dies--he may flee to one of these cities and live; otherwise the avenger of blood might pursue the manslayer in the heat of his anger, and overtake him, because the way is long, and take his life, though he was not deserving of death, since he had not hated him previously. "Therefore, I command you, saying, 'You shall set aside three cities for yourself.'

Deuteronomy 23:7 "You shall not detest an Edomite, for he is your brother; you shall not detest an Egyptian, because you were an alien in his land.

Proverbs 24:29 Do not say, "Thus I shall do to him as he has done to me; I will render to the man according to his work."

Envy

1 Corinthians 13:4 - Love is patient and kind; love does not envy or boast; it his not arrogant.

Psalm 37:1-3 - Fret not yourself because of evildoers; be not envious of wrongdoers! For they will soon fade like the grass and wither like the green herb. Trust in the LORD, and do good; dwell in the land and befriend faithfulness.

Proverbs 14:30 - A tranquil heart gives life to the flesh, but envy makes the bones rot.

Jealousy

Song of Solomon 8:6 - Set me as a seal upon your heart, as a seal upon your arm, for love is strong as death, jealousy is fierce as the grave. Its flashes are flashes of fire, the very flame of the LORD.

Philippians 2:3 - Do nothing from selfish ambition or conceit, but in humility count others more significant than yourselves.

James 3:14-15 - But if you have bitter jealousy and selfish ambition in your hearts, do not boast and be false to the truth. This is not the wisdom that comes down from above, but is earthly, unspiritual, demonic.

James 3:16 - For where jealousy and selfish ambition exist, there will be disorder and every vile practice.

1 Corinthians 3:3 ESV For you are still of the flesh. For while there is jealousy and strife among you, are you not of the flesh and behaving only in a human way?

Hatred

1 John 4:20 - If a man say, I love God, and hateth his brother, he is a liar: for he that loveth not his brother whom he hath seen, how can he love God whom he hath not seen?

1 John 2:9 - He that saith he is in the light, and hateth his brother, is in darkness even until now.

Proverbs 10:12 - Hatred stirreth up strifes: but love covereth all sins.

Matthew 6:15 - But if ye forgive not men their trespasses, neither will your Father forgive your trespasses.

Matthew 5:44 - But I say unto you, Love your enemies, bless them that curse you, do good to them that hate you, and pray for them which despitefully use you, and persecute you;

Proverbs 15:17 - Better [is] a dinner of herbs where love is, than a stalled ox and hatred therewith.

James 1:19-20 - Wherefore, my beloved brethren, let every man be swift to hear, slow to speak, slow to wrath: *(Read More...)*

Ephesians 4:31 - Let all bitterness, and wrath, and anger, and clamour, and evil speaking, be put away from you, with all malice:

Proverbs 10:18 - He that hideth hatred [with] lying lips, and he that uttereth a slander, [is] a fool.

Murder

James 4:2-3 ESV You desire and do not have, so you murder. You covet and cannot obtain, so you fight and quarrel. You do not have, because you do not ask. You ask and do not receive, because you ask wrongly, to spend it on your passions.

Exodus 20:13 You shall not kill.

Leviticus 24:17 And he that kills any man shall surely be put to death.

John 3:12 If I have told you earthly things, and you believe not, how shall you believe, if I tell you of heavenly things?

John 14:15 If you love me, keep my commandments.

Romans 6:23 For the wages of sin is death; but the gift of God is eternal life through Jesus Christ our Lord.

Romans 12:19 Dearly beloved, avenge not yourselves, but rather give place to wrath: for it is written, Vengeance is mine; I will repay, said the Lord.

Romans 13:4 For he is the minister of God to you for good. But if you do that which is evil, be afraid; for he bears not the sword in vain: for he is the minister of God, a revenger to execute wrath on him that does evil.

Revelation 21:8 But the fearful, and unbelieving, and the abominable, and murderers, and fornicators, and sorcerers, and idolaters, and all liars, shall have their part in the lake which burns with fire and brimstone: which is the second death.

PurposeHouse Publishing/ PurposeHouse Ministries / PurposeHouse Christian Counseling

Connect with Us!

Discover the latest tools and encouragement for living on purpose!

Visit (or click) www.purposehouse.net and join our mailing list for the latest blog posts and continued news and previews of other upcoming books.

Visit us on social media

Web:

www.purposehouse.net

YouTube:

http://youtube.com/ministeringpurpose

Facebook:

http://www.facebook.com/purposehouse

Twitter:

http://www.twitter.com/purposehouse

Coming Soon from
PurposeHouse Publishing

Maximize the Multi-:

Soul Stabilizing Devotions for the Multifaceted, Multitasked Woman
by Lenita Reeves

Have you ever asked, "why do I have to do everything myself?" Today's Christian woman is faced with a dilemma and its name is "multi-." While striving to serve the Lord, multiplicities of responsibility vie for her attention. She wrestles to handle it all and at the same time come to grips with her own multifaceted nature. The duty of serving others often overtakes the need for peaceful, quiet times of individual refueling.

Maximize the Multi addresses this issue, facilitates "me time," and anchors Christian women who are dizzy and discombobulated from the winds of multiple responsibilities, talents, and roles. Before a ship sets sail, it must be anchored and refueled. This 30-day devotional is the multitasked, multifaceted woman's necessary, daily dose of anchoring and refueling.

42555654R00046

Made in the USA
Middletown, DE
15 April 2017